T0368696

De-Cluttering

MY JOURNEY TO SELF-LOVE AND A MORE PURPOSEFUL LIFE

PEARL A. MC MASTER

WESTBOW
PRESS®
A DIVISION OF THOMAS NELSON
& ZONDERVAN

This book is a work of non-fiction. Unless otherwise noted, the author and the publisher make no explicit guarantees as to the accuracy of the information contained in this book and in some cases, names of people and places have been altered to protect their privacy.

WestBow Press books may be ordered through booksellers or by contacting:

WestBow Press
A Division of Thomas Nelson & Zondervan
1663 Liberty Drive
Bloomington, IN 47403
www.westbowpress.com
844-714-3454

Because of the dynamic nature of the Internet, any web addresses or links contained in this book may have changed since publication and may no longer be valid. The views expressed in this work are solely those of the author and do not necessarily reflect the views of the publisher, and the publisher hereby disclaims any responsibility for them.

Any people depicted in stock imagery provided by Getty Images are models, and such images are being used for illustrative purposes only. Certain stock imagery © Getty Images.

Cover photo by Lucanus D. Ollivierre

Scripture quotations marked (NIV) are taken from the Holy Bible, NEW INTERNATIONAL VERSION®, NIV® Copyright © 1973, 1978, 1984, 2011 by Biblica, Inc.® Used by permission. All rights reserved worldwide.

ISBN: 979-8-3850-3692-9 (sc)
ISBN: 979-8-3850-3693-6 (e)

Library of Congress Control Number: 2024922547

Print information available on the last page.

WestBow Press rev. date: 01/23/2025

CONTENTS

FOREWORD

....

"De-cluttering: My Journey to Self Love and a More Purposeful Life" is a journey of transformation and discovery. In the hustle and bustle of our daily lives, it's easy to get lost in the chaos of clutter – both physical and mental. But fear not, for you hold in your hands a guide that will illuminate the path to a simpler, more fulfilling existence.

Pearl Mc Master-Mason takes you on a quest to de-clutter not just your surroundings but also your mind and soul. This book isn't just about organizing your living space; it's about reclaiming your time, energy, and most importantly, your self-love and purpose.

As you dive into the wisdom and practical honesty within these chapters, remember that de-cluttering is more than just tidying up – it's a profound act of self-love. You'll unearth the power to let go of what no longer serves you, making room for the joy, purpose, and clarity you deserve.

Your journey to a clutter-free, purpose-filled life begins here. May these words be the catalyst for the positive change you seek and the gateway to a life that radiates with self-love and purpose.

Happy de-cluttering!
Dr. Athalie Caine-Soleyn

ACKNOWLEDGEMENTS

This book is dedicated to and written in memory of my sweet twin sister, Pearla Mc Master-Francis (deceased 2007), my reflection for too short a time; to my father, Jeffeth Mc Master Sr. (deceased 2013) my protector and to my older sister, Yolande Mc Master (killed 2018) my 'beautiful thorn in the flesh'.

This book is also dedicated to my beautiful daughter, Alexa Mason who has been my joy during the writing of this book. To my mother, Henrietta Mc Master my spiritual backbone, my strength and prayer warrior. Thank you to the friends and family who encouraged me throughout this process and to the Holy Spirit who guided me along this path on what to write. God bless you!

INTRODUCTION

Who am I? I am a woman; 49 years old. A christian, brown skin, beautiful, energetic and full of life woman. I consider myself to be well-learned, a professional, yet humorous and witty. I laugh with those who laugh. I cry with those who cry. I am a mother, a divorcee, a sister, a daughter and a friend, but I am tired… tired of doing the same things over and over…tired of 'spinning top in mud'…tired of wishing for this and wishing for that. Oh!! Yes! And I am tired of being broke! I am at a mid-career slump, wishing at times that I had chosen a different career path.

I am always directly or indirectly taking on people's issues, trying to be there for others and in the end I feel deflated, defeated and emotionally drained! I feel as if my life is at a standstill and it is not going anywhere soon. It may not seem like that to my family and friends or even to the people who are looking at me from a distance.

Somehow, I feel that there is still more to my life. More that I have yet to explore. I feel as if I am not truly living out my purpose here on Earth and that there is much more for me to do. Have you ever felt like that?

I came to the realization that life can become so busy and cluttered that we can think ourselves to be doing one thing when really we are doing another. I had to make a change in the way my life was going. I needed to stop... just for a bit...and check myself out. I had to see about me and make some things right for me. Drastic personal life changes had to be made. I embarked on a journey towards self love; a journey towards a more purposeful; and meaningful life. I was no longer satisfied with who I was or where I was at. I wanted to be more!

I'd been *seeing about* others for many years; looking after other people. But what about me? Who had been looking after me? Who was I? What made Pearl Pearl? I knew and I was confident that God loved me, but did I love me? How was I treating me? Over the years, I had poured out so much love to others, but how much love had I poured into me? I had committed to so many people and things, but had I really ever committed to me or to the things that mattered to me? I had forgiven others, but had I forgiven me? Over the years, what were some of the lies I had told myself about relationships, money and people? As I pondered these questions, I wondered, had I really been true to myself?

Here I was, a minister of the gospel, a gospel artiste, a motivational speaker, a mentor, serving a great, big God but lying to myself. I had to de-clutter my life. I had to remove the clutter of lies that I had told myself. In addition, I had to remove the clutter of material things, the clutter of people and the clutter of a spiritual nature. Yes! I had to press the reset button! It was only when I de-cluttered that I would be in a better position to truly begin my journey of self love and living my best life.

Are you willing to take such a journey with me? If you are, then let's get to it!

CHAPTER 1

TOO MUCH STUFF!
(The Clutter of Material Things)

As a librarian, I am trained to always be organized. Every library item has to be put in a systematic order on the shelves, in a filing cabinet, in the pamphlet boxes, and on the computer. The data entry process is quite meticulous just to ensure that data integrity is maintained. So, professionally, my work is about putting things in order or in their proper place. What is not needed or does not fit into the collection is either given away or thrown out.

I have always heard that clutter represents chaos, and certainly, at times, my life felt very chaotic. It was quite ironic that I, a librarian, was about to declutter! I hate clutter! I always want to see things put back in their place. However, as much as I tried to manage the physical things around me, most times stuff just seemed to accumulate. I began to procrastinate in getting things organized and as much as I would give stuff away, things just kept piling up! I had to take action! There was just too much stuff! So, I made a decision to remove from my home any and everything that I did not need or no longer used or wore.

I started decluttering room by room in my house, starting with my bedroom. I removed clothes, shoes, handbags and other accessories, and packed them into big cardboard boxes I acquired from a supermarket. I removed things that were taking up space in the house. I got rid of stuff that I did not even know were there. I took the time to remove some of my daughter's stuff that she no longer needed. I headed to the kitchen and removed food items from the cupboard; food I no longer ate or used. Although it was a daunting task that took me over a week to complete, it was needed and it was worth it. It felt good! It felt liberating! My home felt light too! I now had space for things that mattered.

I also decluttered my work space of irrelevant material, old and non- functioning equipment and files that were no longer in use. I tried my best not to make my office a storage area; as supervisors, we tend to do that. I ensured that the storage room was best used for that function. This process took me just one afternoon to complete.

Making the decision to declutter and organize physical

things around me was an essential and necessary path I took on my journey towards self love. I felt as if I was finally taking charge of the things that concerned me… the things that directly affected me…the things around my space that had become 'eye sores'…the things I had tripped over from time to time. Yes! I de-cluttered it all!

While de-cluttering, I took the opportunity to make a little money by selling clothes and accessories that were either new or in excellent condition (I take care of my things). I also gave to others in my community who were less fortunate than I was. I especially enjoyed and was blessed by my visit to the children's ward of the Milton Cato Memorial Hospital. There, I gave away most of my daughter's teddy bears and stuffed animals to the little boys and girls. It was my second time doing so in recent years. It was such a rewarding feeling! I began to love myself more for doing this, for taking control of what was happening around me. It felt good to make decisions that I wanted to make concerning 'my things' and not have anyone force me to take such action. Yes! I decluttered my things and I love me for it!

CHAPTER 2

NO MORE LIES!
(Clutter of Lies)

Lies may come to you from all different angles of life. Lies always find a way of seeping through the cracks and crevices of our lives from others around us. However, lies can also come from within us. We can directly or indirectly tell ourselves stories and fairytales over and over again.

I realized that there were stories and lies that as a young woman, I'd kept telling myself over the years. I would repeat these lies every time, not knowing the effect they were having on me in the long run. I was not aware that the decisions I was making were the results of the lies I had told myself in the past. As soon as I became aware, I knew that these clutter of lies had to go! For me to live my best life, I had to stop the practice of lying to me! There was now some rethinking I had to do.

These are the lies I'd told myself:

Lie #1: "I had to be there for everybody."

Over the years I'd find myself in situations where I was the sole breadwinner at home. The family would depend on me to pay the bills, buy the food and care for the sick. Many times, I thought that I had to be available to everyone around me. Family, friends, relatives, co-workers, church folks, you name it, I was there. Within myself, I was truly convinced that if I did not avail myself to help others in times of need it meant that I was somehow being a selfish, sinful woman! How dare I refuse to help others?!! How were they going to look at me? If I said 'no' what would they say about me? For years, these were all the questions that I pondered time and time again. In hindsight, I could see that, sometimes, I was not even in a position to help, but yet I could not say 'no'. No matter how hard I tried, I always found myself saying 'yes'.

When I did not have it to give, I would borrow money to assist those who asked. Even when I was tired or sick, I would overextend myself to others in so many ways. What was even worse was that many times, my efforts were not received "with thanks" or they went unnoticed. I have come to the realization that my saying 'yes' to everybody was a lie I'd been telling myself for years! Now, I tell myself that I can say 'no'.

I can say 'no' without feeling guilty or feeling that I have offended someone. I can now say 'no' with a big fat smile on my face and not think twice about it. I realize I can help some people but not everyone. Trying to be there for everyone only left me feeling stressed, dejected, emotionally tired and at times very frustrated! I made a decision to choose who I wish to help and be there for. I also made it a habit to seek God's guidance as to whom I should be there for.

I no longer allow this lie to take up 'residence' in my mind. It no longer has a hold on me or dictates my decision as to whom I choose to help.

Lie #2: "I can't make it without a husband/man."

As a Christian woman, being taught the scriptures growing up, I learned that the man is the head of the home and that he is responsible for providing for his family (1Timothy 5:8). I strongly believe that this biblical structure is a strong element in any Christian home with a nuclear family.

However, the common reality is that there are so

many single women raising children by themselves. It is also very clear that it has become quite a frequent happening even within the church as well.

Growing up, I'd always dreamed of marrying, having a husband with children and having the support of my husband in various ways. Having the financial, emotional, physical and spiritual support of a husband is paramount in any marriage and when as a wife/woman you lose that support, whether through separation, divorce or death, you feel less than adequate, as if your world has ended.

One of the lies I'd told myself over the years was that I would not be able to make it without a husband/man in my life. When my divorce became final in 2013, I said to myself, "that's it girl, you on your own". I was disappointed that the marriage had not worked out; it lasted only two years. I was left sad, depressed, hurt, rejected and I had no clue what was about to happen next for me and my baby girl. I found myself alone with my baby and no husband.

It was at that point that the lies began to creep into my psyche. I kept telling myself that I could not move forward on my own. For the next seven years, I kept repeating this lie. This lie caused me to make decisions regarding relationships and friendships that I regret. It's a lie that caused me to become vulnerable in relationships that left me hurting and feeling rejected. I would always joke to my friends that my next husband should be "ah ole white man wid plenty money". It sounded funny then but I was dead serious! That's how far I had gone with the lie that I could not handle life by myself.

As women we look to men for a level of security in relationships and when that is gone, we are left in vulnerable positions, wondering and hoping when we will find another to love and support us and give us that sense of security we so need. I had to remove that lie from within me. I had to tell myself that I am enough and well capable of taking care of me. I began to speak truth to me. My mindset had to change.

I started to affirm myself every day. I told myself:

"I am beautiful."
"I am gifted"
"I am loved."
"I am intelligent."
"I am strong."
"I am enough!"

I focused on who I am and who God has allowed me to become. Looking back now, I am happy to say that I have actually made it to this point without a man by my side.

I trusted God all the way. It is God that has kept and sustained me every day since my divorce. It is God who has given me the strength to push forward and encourage other women who might be feeling the same way. I have learned the art of being alone but not lonely. I have decided to love myself and not wait for a man to come along and love me. If one does come along, then he would be a 'bonus' for me.

Lie #3: "I will always struggle financially"

This was one of my biggest lies I told myself. I grew up with parents who were not rich but who always made sure that my siblings and I were taken care of. My dad use to work on a shrimp trawler based in Trinidad and Tobago and he would sail to different countries to fish for shrimp. My mother was a seamstress, plying her trade at home. They both tried their best to give us an education and to ensure that we grew up as good citizens.

I can recall that there were times when we did not always have enough, especially when my dad decided to come off the seas for good. I was 13 years old then and had just entered Girls' High School. There were times I didn't have 'recess' and stayed in the classroom pretending to do homework until the bell rang. There were times when I had just bread and butter with lime juice for lunch, but no one knew. I was sort of embarrassed by it. I remember when my mother would "turn over" my school uniform skirt for the next school term just so that she did not have to buy a new one. As a teenager, I had no idea what it meant to have a lot.

As a young woman, I also knew what it felt like to be low on cash, to not have enough food in the cupboard or refrigerator. I settled for the lie that I would always struggle financially. The fact that I had a stable job did not matter; it did not make a difference to me. I still struggled!

I became so comfortable in my sad financial state that I kept telling myself that this was my lot in life. Unless I found a rich man to marry, I was always going to struggle financially. I settled into the life of living 'pay cheque to pay cheque!' I would normally say the words; 'I does get pay under fan" or 'my money have hole in it". I did not know that these words had a negative impact on me financially.

In reality, I was making detrimental financial decisions. I never budgeted. I made financial investments that caused me to lose substantial amounts of money. I ended up with loans here, there, and everywhere! I maxed out my credit card on two separate occasions. This one might shock you, but I was not consistent in my tithe giving at church. It came to a point where at the end of each month; all I could do was service my loans and pay the utility bills, with just a little left over to buy food and gas. Looking back, I often wonder how I made it. It was only by the grace of God. He was still merciful to me.

So, I struggled financially for years and I became comfortable struggling. Once I made ends meet, I was good! Such a lie! I kept lying to myself that this was just the way it was going to be. I listened to sermons on prosperity and abundance and somehow they did not resonate with me. I had to remove this clutter of a lie that told me that I would always struggle financially.

I began to replace this lie with the truth that I did not have to struggle and that I did not have to live "pay cheque to pay cheque". I not only began to think differently and speak positively, but I followed up with action.

So I began budgeting monthly; I started practicing a level of minimalism (simple lifestyle). This meant that I went out less, I bought fewer clothes, I decided to go back to my natural hair, which meant that I visited the hair salon less and I took care of my own hair. It didn't last long though; I just couldn't manage the natural hair so I settled for a short relaxed hair style with a pixie cut.

I only bought the food that I needed and started a little back yard garden with my family. I also planned ways to begin my debt free process. I began to pay off small loans and work my way up to the bigger loans. I doubled payments on my credit card (It was paid off!). I also made a decision to charge for my services as a singer and speaker at conferences etc. I am still working on giving my tithes consistently (do not judge me!).

This is a journey that is continuing and has really made a financial difference in my life. Even now, I see and feel the effects of the financial changes that I had to make. Sometimes, I fall back into bad habits but I quickly pick myself up and go again. I am capable of prospering financially. I am capable of acquiring wealth! I may not be rich, but I am definitely not struggling! Praise Jesus!

Lie#4: "If I treat people well, they will treat me well too"

In general, I have always characterized myself as a good, kind, person. Over the years, I have always reached out to others to help in whichever way I can. I have mentored young girls; I have taken them into my home. I have tried my best to positively impact others while on my job, at my church and in my own community. There were times when I selflessly gave my time, money, knowledge and opportunities to others. In return I received slander, ungratefulness, curse words, negativisms, criticisms and the like.

I grew up telling myself that once I was good to you then you would be good to me. While that may be the case for some, not all people are the same. I sometimes found myself asking the question, "What could I have possibly done to this person or that person? All I did was to treat them well and this is how they treat me in return?"

My mistake was that I expected too much from people. Sometimes I thought that the persons I treated well were a lot like me. I expected them to treat me right in return; however, that seldom was the case. This type of expectation is especially frequent in relationships with a partner, a family member and also among friends. It can cause you to become hurt and discouraged in life.

So, I decided to get rid of this lie! People are not going to treat you well because you treat them well! The quicker I understood that, the better it was for me. I no longer had expectations of others. I did what I could to help without looking for anything in return. If I keep expecting good from others and do not receive it, then it is going to leave me frustrated. Jesus says "...no one is good except God alone." (Mark 19:18). I must leave room for disappointment in this life. De-cluttering the lies was all part of my journey towards self love and living a more purposeful life.

No more lies! I was done!

CHAPTER 3

THEY GOT TO GO!
(Clutter of People)

Today, we live in a world where we are surrounded by so many people. Everywhere you look; there are friends, family, acquaintances, co- workers and groups.

There are all types of people. There are those family and friends you wish would only come around once a year! Those friends and family who never get tired of calling on you! Yes! Acquaintances and groups that just waste your time! Yes! You know what I am talking about. There are endless meetings that lead to nowhere. Friends that get on your last nerve from time to time; and relatives who come to visit and never leave! Oh yes! Some serious de-cluttering has to take place. They've got to go!

I had to think long and hard about the people I

wanted around me. I needed to remove the negative energy that was emanating from some persons. I knew, exactly at this point, what I wanted in my space and what I no longer wanted to disrupt and frustrate me during this journey towards self love. So I began the de-cluttering of people!

1. Family and friends that drained me emotionally and physically

I knew for my own sanity, I had to remove friends and family that drained me emotionally. It was not a hard decision for me to make. I already knew beyond a shadow of a doubt such persons had to go! I was already prepared for the different reactions I would receive. I was prepared for those who would feel 'offended'. I was prepared for those who would be angry and upset and of course those who had no clue and it really did not matter to them which way the coin fell.

I made the decision to let go of the one-sided friendships. You know those friendships where you are the one making most of the effort to be friends. You are always the one to make contact and hang out on their terms, listening to their problems while they don't seem to care about your issues. They would take your time but would seldom want to give back theirs! Those friends had to go!

I chose also to let go of relatives who always expected me to drop my life for them. They expect me to put their needs before my needs. I had to declutter family who only found me important when I had money to give them. They are the family and relatives who would never ask, "how you are doing?" and always, "what you have to give?" Yes! The takers! Always wanting to take from you but never willing to give back. They had to go!!

2. People who are not trustworthy

I chose to let go of persons who had proven that they are not trustworthy. When persons break your trust, it can be a shocking and devastating experience, especially if you have been friends for a long time. It can become challenging to break off such friendships. There are also those persons who become friends and acquaintances with you for different reasons. They may have their own sinister motives for the friendship. Be aware of such persons!

Over the years, I have had to deal with people who broke my trust. I would get upset, express my feelings and after a while forgive them. Then the cycle would begin again! I came to the realization that such persons did not have my best interest at heart. They were only in the friendship to see what information they could gather about me or any situation in which I was involved. Most times, those friendships caused me much pain and hurt. I had to end such friendships.

Over the years I had to deal with coworkers who were not trustworthy. You know those coworkers who smile with you and then "chop you down" when you are not in their presence. Yes! Those coworkers who pretend that they are on your side and when it really matters you find yourself being "thrown under the bus" by them or not getting the support you needed. You just don't know which way it will go when it comes to such people. Yep!! They had to go!

3. People who are contentious, negative and always complaining

These are the people who bring absolutely no "joy to my soul"! It was a necessary action that I had to take in getting rid of such persons from my life, if I wanted to live a life of peace, joy and drama-free!

These are the people that get offended easily. They always see the negative side of things and no matter how much you try to convince them otherwise, they just do not make the effort to see the positive.

These are the people who complain about everything.

I mean e-ve-ry thing! They would complain about who is on their team, the air conditioning being too hot or too cold. They would complain about the work being too hard or too much. They would complain about the brother or the sister, and what he/she is wearing, or not wearing. They are the ones who always want to argue. Their mouths are the loudest in the room and they are ever present in some drama or "melee." I believe you may have come across that contentious person at some point in your life. I have come across quite a few.

I met them in my community, at school, on the job, and yes! At church too! I promised myself that these are the people I would avoid at all cost. Proverbs 27:15 tells me that, "A constant dripping on a day of steady rain and a contentious woman [man] are alike." Imagine, King Solomon in Proverbs 21:9 alluded to the fact that, "It is better to live in a corner of a roof than in a house with a contentious woman." This is the type of energy I no longer wanted around me. For me to be my best self and to embark on my journey toward self love, they had to go!!

In de-cluttering such people, I did not prepare a list of talking points, or practice any conversation. I just simply let them go. It may seem a drastic thing to do, however, my life depended on it!

4. People with too much baggage

I have formed some lasting relationships with some kind, wonderful, loving and just simply nice human beings. However, what I have noticed is that no matter how wonderful people are, we all have some baggage hiding under the bed! Baggage shows up from past friendships and relationships, and help to destroy new relationships. Emotional baggage shows up, financial baggage shows up, even spiritual baggage finds its way into the mix! It's just too much baggage!

I have had to be on my Ps and Qs with persons in my life who, often through no fault of their own, became stagnant in the friendship because their heart was too full of pain and hurts from their past, pain that they could not seem to get past and found it difficult to overcome. These friendships became a burden to me. Their baggage became my burden. I felt as if I was not enjoying the kind of healthy, loving friendship I deserved. We all have our baggage, but some people seem to enjoy toting their baggage!

These are the people who serve up the 'blame game.' They often believe that the cause of their problem is someone else. They blame their parents, their school, their job or their ex for their messed up life and why they cannot move forward. These are the people with control issues. They would normally want to control and manage things for fear of 'not feeling safe.' I tell you, they end up manipulating and smothering you as you get close to them. You cannot have healthy relationships with such persons. They are the very persons who do not like to receive criticism. They become sulky, defensive and angry when you offer criticism. They are forever stuck in their past and fail to enjoy the present or look towards the future. This can be a very frustrating experience for anybody who has relationships with such people. "Me carn' tek dem friendship dey!" I had a girlfriend with whom I always "knocked heads" because of the amount of baggage she carried. It affected our relationship terribly, to the point where I had begun to become wary of her. I knew there and then that this was not how I was supposed to feel. I sensed that something was wrong. The truth of the matter is that her baggage was just too much for me after a while and as much as I wanted to be there for her, I had to make the decision to pull back!

Over the years I have tried my best to hold on to people with baggage, fearing they would harm themselves for whatever reasons (it did not take much) but it began to become too much for me. My journey towards self love could not include them. They had to go!

5. Groups that wasted my time

I strongly believe in getting involved in civil society. I believe it is important to make some level of contribution to my community and country on a whole. We all have a civic duty to do so. At the risk of sounding like your past Social Studies teacher, here is a little advice for you. Being a part of different groups and organizations provide an avenue for you to help others in positive ways. It also facilitates your creativity and helps you to grow your mental and social skills. Over the years, I have been a part of groups/organizations, making my contribution and learning different skills along the way.

However, there came a time when there was just too much happening. I found myself involved in so many different groups doing different activities. I was attending all kinds of meetings here and there. I realized that some of these groups were not helping me in serving the purpose to which I was called and I had to quickly leave these groups.

Some of the groups certainly wasted my time. Useless meetings were held with no way forward. Group leaders were neither here nor there! Some groups could not settle on specific goals or objectives. Persons could not agree on the simplest of things! Those groups had to go! It was becoming a challenge trying to keep up with these different organizations. I believe too that I would have outlived my time and purpose for such organizations. It made no sense to me to continue being part of a group that contributed more stress to my life and no longer served a particular purpose for me. The groups that wasted my time had to be cut off!

Persons labeled me ungrateful for leaving groups and organizations. Persons were downright offended. I have no regrets! It was just too much! So, I kindly resigned and exited! In doing so, I now had more time available for me to write my songs, study the word of God, and write speeches that would motivate and encourage others. After de-cluttering the time wasting groups, I had more time on my hands to do the things I loved and enjoyed. I took the time to invest in me!

CHAPTER 4

MY SPIRIT SENSE!
(Clutter that negatively affects my spirit)

In this world today, so many voices and opinions compete for our attention. They come from all different avenues, some positive and some negative. However, I'd made a decision to remove everything that negatively affected my spirit. So, the things that distracted and caused me to lose focus, I knew I had to get rid of them in order to live my best life and continue my journey of self love. I de-cluttered:

1. Anger and Bitterness

The scripture says "Be angry and sin not..." (Ephesians 4:26) I understood those words to mean that as a believer I could be angry. I could experience the emotions of anger.

However, what I could not do is express my anger in such a way that it would cause me to sin. At one point, the anger that I felt consumed and controlled who I was. It affected my spirit and my actions toward others.

For me, my anger stemmed from different places and circumstances. I was angry and bitter over past relationships, especially over the fact that my marriage did not work out years ago. Looking back now, I was so angry at my husband back then that it led to my divorce. I was angry at the fact that he was not with us as a family. I was angry about my financial situation at the time, angry about the fact that under certain circumstances, I was forced to move back to my parents' house to live, and angry that I was raising our daughter by myself. This anger and bitterness continued for a couple years. It was not until I prayed specifically about it and made a decision not to be bitter anymore, that I got past all the anger and God was able to take all those negative emotions away. I realized that for my life to have purpose and meaning, I had to release all the anger that was built up inside me. It was a lot of work; I had to forgive and forget. God was able to turn things around. Even though my ex husband and I did not get back together, we remain good friends and continue to co-parent our daughter.

On 8th September 2018, the worst thing that could have happened to me, did. One of my older sisters was murdered in my village not too far from where I was living. When I received the news of her death, I was flabbergasted. I was numb. I was an emotional wreck! I'd never experienced so many emotions at any one time in my life before. The emotion that consumed me the most was anger. I was angry at myself, I hadn't protected her. I was angry at my sister for not listening to me when I spoke to her about being on the streets during late hours. I was angry at the person/persons who'd committed such a gross act against my sister (she was raped and murdered). I was angry that my father was no longer alive, for if he was, I strongly believed that my sister would still be here with me as the killers would have thought twice before harming her. I was angry at the village, angry that we had such wicked persons living among us. I was angry at the police for not finding the killer/killers. I was angry at the country whenever there was abuse or killings of women. I felt that we were failing to protect our women. I was angry at God for allowing all these things to happen to me. I was just angry, and the anger consumed me terribly! It began to control my thoughts and actions. For weeks I could not drive past the area where my sister's body was found. I took a different route. I could not look at certain men in the village who I felt had raped my sister; I just wanted to hit them with my car! I did not want to speak or be around anyone. I just wanted to be left alone. I was bitter!

As a Christian, it was one of the most challenging times in my life. I had to deal with my anger. It became too much for me to handle, and it descended into depression. I decided to seek professional help. I had to learn to process and channel my anger positively. I had to get away from the scene of it all and find time for myself to meditate and really seek God for inner healing. It took me a while to overcome my anger but with prayer, counseling and support, I was able to release my anger. Over time, the very people with whom I was angry, I had to forgive them, including myself. It was the only way I was able to move on to living my best life. Let me caution you at this point. Never allow anger to get to the point where it consumes you and controls your life. It is an emotion that we all will experience at some point in our lives but you must be able to process your anger and channel it in the right way. My anger had to go; it was cluttering my mind and affecting my spirit in a negative way.

2. Unforgiveness

I find that one of the hardest things I have had to do over the years was to forgive people who'd hurt me in one way or the other. As a Believer, I thought this would have been 'a breeze' but it was no easy task. Unforgiveness was a clutter within me that too often showed up in my life. I had to remove all unforgiveness that was present within me.

I was reminded in Colossians 3:13 to *"Bear with each other and forgive whatever grievances you may have against one another. Forgive as the Lord forgave you."* There were women who I had to forgive, you know, those women that have no respect for your relationship with your significant other. Yes! Those women! I had to forgive friend and relatives who just used and abused me from time to time, those relatives who were unjust in their actions towards me. I had to forgive men who hurt me in past relationships (hmmm, these were the hardest to forgive!). I had to forgive persons who lied on me. Yes! Unforgiveness had to go! It had become a stumbling block for me. I always tripped over clutters of unforgiveness until I got it right. I began to practice the art of forgiving. I began to forgive quickly because the longer I took to forgive, the harder it became for me to do so. So I forgave quickly and released persons immediately, which worked well for me. Unforgiveness would not be a part of me going forward, it had to go!

3. Negative opinions, criticism and suggestions

Without sounding too much like your parents, let me emphasize here, that one of the worst things you can do to yourself is to listen to negative opinions, criticisms and suggestions from others. Your friends might think it's all good coming from them, but most times their opinions are self-centered and do not benefit you in anyway. There are those who will always have something negative to say about you. There are those who will never see any good in you, for whatever reasons they may have. The trick is not to internalize people's opinions and criticisms about you. Try not to take them personally and let them be a catalyst for you pushing forward in your journey of life. I had to learn to block and tune out people's opinion about me.

I purposely chose to stop focusing on people's criticisms and opinions of me. It was becoming a distraction in my life. People's opinions were causing me to lose focus on the things that really mattered; my family, my job, and my ministry. People's opinions and criticisms were another clutter I had to get rid of. I chose to no longer internalize them. They were a bother to my spirit man. They had to go!

4. De-cluttering social media activities

At this stage in my life, I frankly believe that it is not necessary for me to be on every social media platform there is. Don't get me wrong! To each his own! For me, social media was becoming a total distraction in my life. I even forgot some of the platforms that I was on existed, yet I had accounts on all of them. I remember while reading for my Masters degree in Information Science, I had to create accounts on these social media platforms as part of my studies. I created Blogs, accounts on X (formerly Twitter), LinkedIn, Instagram, Facebook, YouTube channel and in addition news forums. After my studies, it became overwhelming to keep up with these social media platforms. Mind you, I now had WhatsApp and many different WhatsApp groups to contend with! It was becoming a burden to keep up! At this point, I looked at which platform worked for me and I decided to de-activate the others. I also cleaned up my contact list on my phone, email and FaceBook friends list. Some people had to be blocked and 'unfriended'!

I also felt that I had to avoid certain conversations that some friends wanted to engage in on social media; such as gossiping, slandering and belittling others. These conversations are not pleasing to God. I tried my best to avoid them at all costs. If I sensed a conversation was heading down that road, I quickly tried to change the subject or come up with an excuse to end the conversation. I would even go as far as to directly say to friends, I do not want to talk about this or that.

Social media has taken up so much of our time; it's amazing how long people spend on social media platforms. Like, share, subscribe, retweet, react, this is how social media manifests itself in people's lives today. According to statistics, an average of 2 ½ hours is spent on social media each day (Kemp, 2024). I had to discipline myself regarding the use of social media platforms and declutter them from my life.

5. De-cluttering what I watch and listen to on the TV and Radio

In this age of information, so many things can come at you at any one time. It is therefore important that you be mindful of what you look at on television and what you listen to on the radio.

When it comes to the information that you receive on a day to day basis, you have to be careful what you look at and what you listen to. All sorts of information will come to you in different ways; via music, news, politics, talk shows, game shows, movies, reality shows, documentaries, religious programs, you name it. At some point or the other, your ears and eyes will be exposed to such. It's the age we are living in.

Any and everybody is creating content online and some content may be educational and informative and may benefit me in some way. However, others have proven to be violent, racist, degrading to women and of no personal benefit to me. Let me not forget the content that is just downright silly and is a waste of my time here on earth!

I am a lover of news, especially international news. I always want to know what is happening around the world. I like to keep myself well informed on current world issues. However, my friends close to me will tell you that I am obsess with the United States of America's president, Number 45! Yes! Mr. Donald Trump himself! From the time he announced his candidacy for president of the USA, until recently, I was always looking at or listening to anything regarding Trump! Yes, it was bad, I know! I must admit it. I am sure some of you are smiling at this point for you may have found yourself in this same situation, being so fascinated by the fact that America had elected Mr. Trump as president, and wanting to see how his presidency was going to play out. So I watched news, press conferences, ads, documentaries, memes, songs about him; you name it, I watched it. I read books about him and I followed him on Twitter too!

Eventually, all this information I was taking in about this president became a big distraction and evoked all kinds of emotions in me. I had to slowly lessen and lessen what I watched. I believe that it was my love for politics that caused me to become so caught up in American politics. My dad and I used to talk local politics all the time; it was one of the things that kept us close. He loved his politics. Politics was the last thing we discussed just before he died. After his death, I choose not to discuss politics with anyone else, and so with his death, my love for politics died as well. Strangely enough, it was resurrected with the presidential candidacy of Donald Trump in the USA. I knew this was something my Dad and I would have enjoyed talking about. After 2 years of constantly looking at Trump, I had to stop. I had to de-clutter. Trump was not contributing to my best self at all! The process of de-cluttering from Trump took a while. It was no easy task! I really found him entertaining; my new reality show! My friends and family were so fed up of me talking about President Trump. They were not afraid to give me "that look" or to express their displeasure to me, "Yuh nah fed up ah Trump?", 'I don't want to hear bout Trump" and the best one for me was, "yuh not watching no Trump pon me TV." It's no wonder a whole page of this book is about him. I am still a work in progress, please do not judge me!

In all seriousness, I had to come to the realization, that what I listened to and watched on various media had to be evaluated and I had to make a conscious effort to de-clutter those things that were having a negative effect on me mentally, psychologically and spiritually. Even some religious programs, I stopped looking at. They were just sending the wrong message to viewers. News items no longer just gave the news, but I was also bombarded with other people's opinions and views about the facts also. It was becoming too much for me. So instead, I lessened what I watched and listened to. I began to read more. You may think that as a Librarian, I was an avid reader, not necessarily. Sorry to disappoint you there! Now, I choose to read books that edify me spiritually, books that educate and inform me. And yes! I began to write more! I wrote poems, songs and books. All of this was coupled with my reading and studying of the most important book of all, my Bible!

6. Learn to say no!

As my music ministry began to grow, one of the things that I quickly became aware of, and was not about to do was to be in every gospel concert or every religious activity that came my way. Personally, I took that stand because of what used to happen to me in earlier years. I was active in everything concerning church! Gospel concerts, church rallies, marches, crusades, youth camps/ retreats, conventions and while I was no dancer, I ended up in dance groups too.

I can be quite dramatic at times, so it was only natural that I would find myself in drama groups as well. I was mostly involved with youth groups and believe me, leading young people can be quite challenging for any young woman. I am sure some of you can identify with me. I was just going and going like the 'Energizer Bunny' on TV. There was no 'off' switch for me when it came to church activities and gospel shows. At one point in my life, I would religiously hop on a plane to Barbados to attend the Barbados Gospel Fest every year for over a period of 10 years, just to take in various gospel concerts happening on a weekend. Like old people would say, "I just wanted to hear a pan knock and I was gone!" Yes, that was me.

As young and healthy as I was, I slowly began to burn out. Everybody wanted Pearl to be a part of this and that. "Pearl can you sing a song for us?" While I greatly appreciated the opportunities, I was reminded that I could not do it all. In recent years, my ministry no longer just entailed singing but it grew into other things. I am now involved in preaching, motivational speaking and giving feature addresses. I also found myself praying and counseling others who requested it. I deeply realized at this point that I could not move without the leading of the Holy Spirit. There are those, even in the church body, who do not understand my decision not to run with every gospel or Christian activity that is brought to me. At times, I had to practice saying 'no'. If I am not led to do it, then I won't do it. Some people may call it being selfish, but 'to each his own.' I want to make sure that whatever I do in ministry is God-driven and not of my own selfish need or agenda. Saying 'no' to some Christian activities does not make me any less a Christian.

I vowed never to allow anyone to plant a 'guilt trip' on me because I chose not to be part of a particular event or I did not attend a Christian function at a particular point. I would caution you here that you have to be spiritually mature enough and be much disciplined in order to pull this off, especially in the culture we live in today. Why? Because people will judge you for it!

In order for me to live out the purpose and plans God has for me and in order for me to continue this journey of self love and to be my best self, I had to de-clutter all these things from within and around me. I am passionate in everything; when I talk, when I sing, when I preach, when I move! It takes my whole being to put myself out there and minister the gospel of Christ to others and to do so, I must be whole.

If I am going to minister healing, I must be healed, if I am going to minister forgiveness, I must forgive, if I'm going to minister love, I too must love. Hence the reason for this journey towards self love. I have discovered a lot about myself during this journey. Some things I liked others I did not. I try my best each and every day, with the help of God, to improve on me and be my best self.

Thank you for taking this journey with me and thanks to the Holy Spirit who led me during the writing of this book. May this book inspire you to take your own journey towards self love and understand that your life can be so much more if you allow God to fulfill His purpose in you! God bless you!

REFERENCE

Kemp, Simone. 2024. *The time we spend on social media.* DataReportal. https://datareportal.com/reports/digital-2024-deep-dive-the-time-we-spend-on-social-media

Anon, (n.d.). *the bible.*

Printed in the United States
by Baker & Taylor Publisher Services